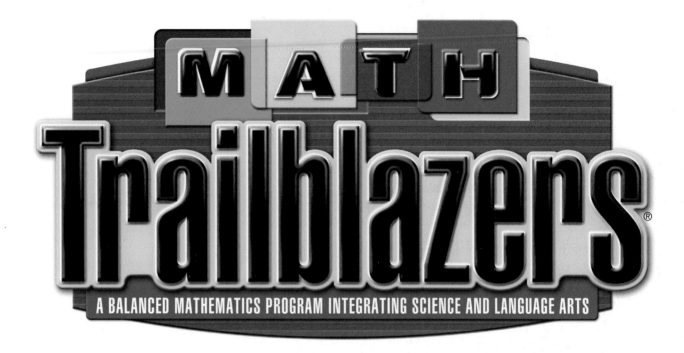

MATH Trailblazers®

A BALANCED MATHEMATICS PROGRAM INTEGRATING SCIENCE AND LANGUAGE ARTS

Adventure Book

THIRD EDITION

KENDALL/HUNT PUBLISHING COMPANY
4050 Westmark Drive   Dubuque, Iowa 52002

A TIMS® Curriculum
University of Illinois at Chicago

MATH TRAILBLAZERS®

Dedication

This book is dedicated to
the children and teachers who
let us see the magic in their classrooms
and to our families who wholeheartedly
supported us while we searched for
ways to make it happen.

The TIMS Project

  **UIC** The University of Illinois at Chicago

The original edition was based on work supported by the National Science Foundation under grant No. MDR 9050226 and the University of Illinois at Chicago. Any opinions, findings, and conclusions or recommendations expressed in this publication are those of the authors and do not necessarily reflect the views of the granting agencies.

Printed in the United States of America

1 2 3 4 5 6 7 8 9 10   11 10 09 08 07

Table of Contents

You Can't Do That

Yü the Great
A Chinese Legend

So, Yü and Yi traveled all over China gathering data. They measured the land and the rivers, the hills and the swamps. They studied the kinds of soil in each part of the empire. Then, Yü made a map of the empire. He marked the four mountains. He showed the sea, the rivers, the swamps, and the lakes.

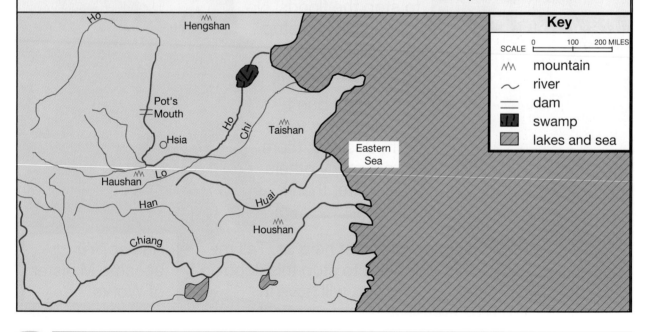

Everywhere in the empire, Yü measured the land and the rivers.

He made new places for the rivers to flow to the sea. He made swamps into lakes and made other lakes deeper. Then, the rivers did not overflow. Yü and Yi worked hard for many years. The people cooperated to make the land a better place to live.

One day, when Yü was working on the Lo River, an amazing thing happened. A giant turtle crawled out of the river. On the turtle's back was a strange design.

Yü and Yi studied the design on the turtle's back for a long time. They found many patterns in the design. They called the design Lo-shu.

This design holds great wisdom. Look how perfectly balanced it is in every way. This design can help us make a Great Plan for the empire.

Yes! The empire should be balanced and orderly like this design.

Inspired by the balanced design of Lo-shu, Yü created a Great Plan for the empire. Yü's Great Plan told how the people could be made happy and peaceful. It explained how to make the government strong and fair. Yü divided the empire into nine parts, just as Lo-shu was divided into nine parts.

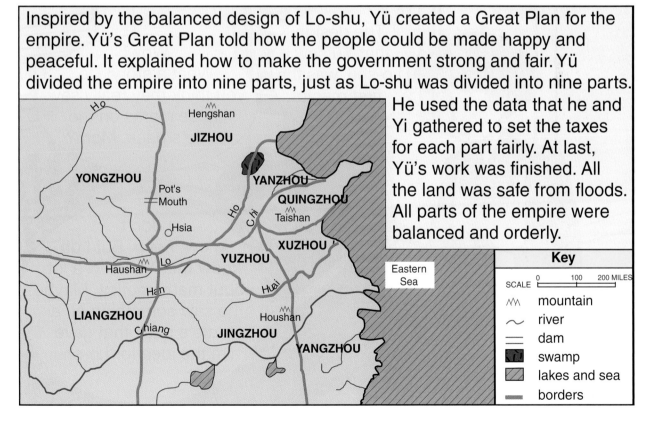

He used the data that he and Yi gathered to set the taxes for each part fairly. At last, Yü's work was finished. All the land was safe from floods. All parts of the empire were balanced and orderly.

Key

SCALE 0 100 200 MILES

~~~ mountain
~ river
= dam
swamp
lakes and sea
borders

Years later, Yao died, and Shun became emperor. Yü became Shun's helper. When Shun died later, Yü became emperor. Yü was the first of a great line of emperors, the Hsia.

For all his work building the empire, Yü was called Great. He was the only Chinese emperor called Great.

The design that Yü saw, Lo-shu, was the first magic square.

Wow! What a story! Do you think they really saw those marks on the turtle's back, Mom?

I don't know, Feng. But I do know that Yü knew a lot about mathematics. Maybe he saw something on a turtle's back that gave him the idea for Lo-shu.

The Haunted House

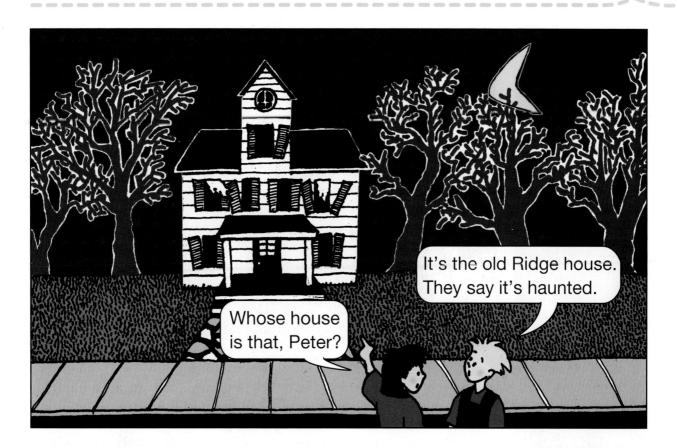

The next day, bright and early.

Let's try the second floor.

Okay.

Look!

A footprint in the dust.

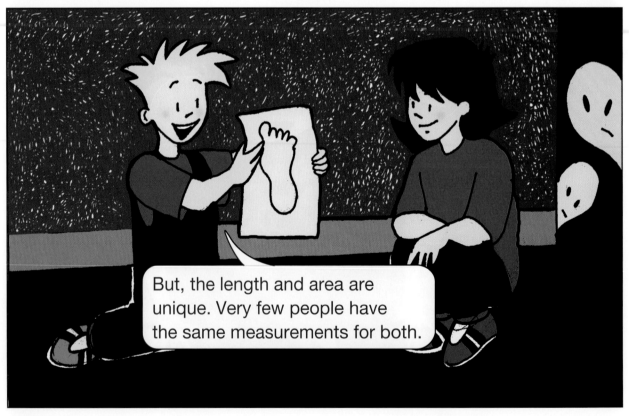

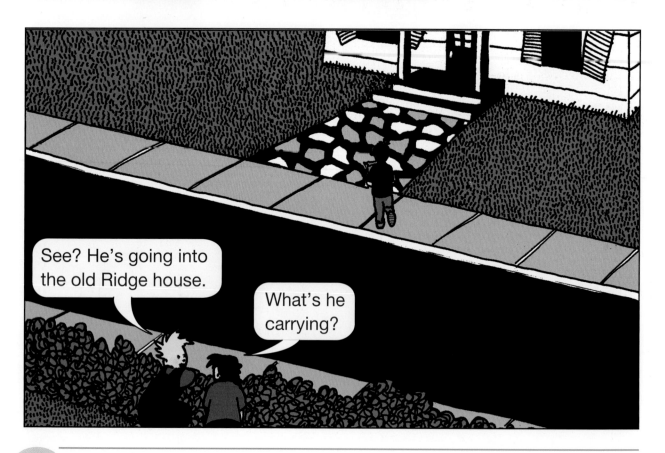

Leonardo the Blockhead

Over 800 years ago in the Italian city of Pisa, a young boy, Leonardo, watches his father, Bonacci, at work.

"What are you doing, Father?" asks Leonardo.

Bonacci answers, "Peter of Rome has just sent me one thousand three hundred thirty-eight bags of flour. Before this, I had two thousand one hundred three bags. Now, I must find how many I have altogether."

"Can't you just count all the bags?" asks young Leonardo.

"That's a good idea, son, but it wouldn't work," answers Bonacci. "If we tried to count them all at one time, we would probably lose track since all the bags look exactly alike. Even if we could count each one, it would take a very long time. What I really need to do is add the number of Peter's bags to the number of my own."

"How do you do that, Father?" asks Leonardo.

"I use an abacus, son. Watch, I'll show you how. First, we put pebbles representing my bags of flour on the lines."

"What do those letters mean, Father?"

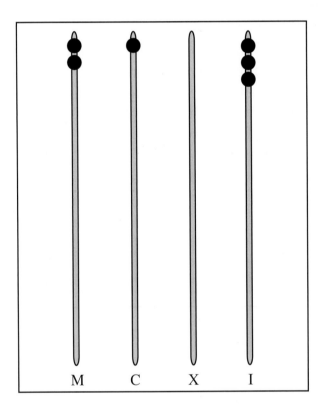

M   C   X   I

"The M is for *milli,* which means thousands. The C is for *centi,* which means hundreds. The X means tens. The I means ones," explains Bonacci.

"So, the two pebbles on the M line mean two thousand, the one pebble on the C line means one hundred, and the three pebbles on the I line mean three. Altogether, the abacus shows two thousand one hundred three. We write 'MMCIII' for the number of my bags."

"Next, we must add Peter's bags to my own. Since he sent me one thousand three hundred thirty-eight bags of flour, we add one pebble on the M line (for one thousand), three more pebbles on the C line (for three hundred), three pebbles on the X line (for thirty), and eight pebbles on the I line (for eight). We write 'MCCCXXXIIIIIIII' for the number of Peter's bags."

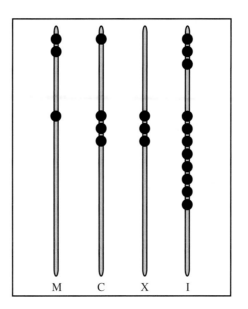

MMCIII

+ MCCCXXXIIIIIIII

"Is that all?" asks Leonardo.
"Is the number of all the bags MMMCCCCXXXIIIIIIIIIIII?"

"Not quite," replies Bonacci. "There are too many pebbles on the I line. You see, we can never have more than nine pebbles on any line. So, we need to remove ten of the pebbles on the I line and add a single pebble on the X line."

"Why do we do that?"

"Because the ten I pebbles are ten ones," answers Bonacci. "We can trade ten ones for one ten. Then, we can put the one ten on the X line. So now, we know there are three thousand four hundred forty-one bags of flour altogether. We write 'MMMCCCCXXXXI.'"

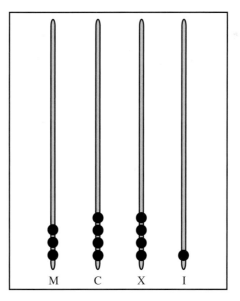

MMCIII

+ MCCCXXXIIIIIIII

MMMCCCCXXXXI

So, Leonardo learns the abacus and helps his father with the business.

But soon, Leonardo and his family move to Bugia in North Africa. There, the young boy has Arab teachers.

Leonardo's Arab teachers write numbers in a different way. They learned their way from the Hindus, a people who live in India.

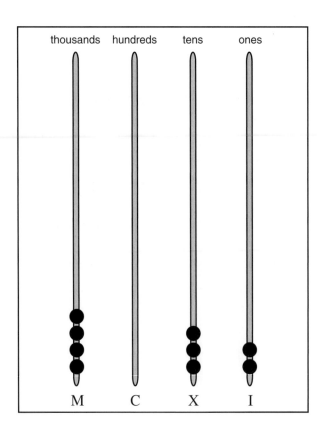

"So, we write '4032' for four thousand thirty-two," explains Kalil, Leonardo's first Arab teacher. "We can show it on an abacus like this."

"Oh, I see!" says Leonardo.

"Instead of MMMMXXXII, you write '4032.' The 4 means four thousand because it is in the thousands place; the 0 means we have no hundreds; the 3 means thirty since it is in the tens place; and the 2 means two since it is in the ones place. That's easier!"

Later, Leonardo tries to explain the Arabic numbers to his father.

"So, Father, if I write '301,' it means three hundred one. The 3 means three hundreds; the 0 means no tens; and the 1 means one," says Leonardo. "But if I write '103,' it means one hundred three."

But his father says, "How can that be? How can this 3 mark sometimes be three hundred and other times be just three? Three hundred is CCC, and three is III! Please don't confuse me with all these newfangled numbers."

Soon, the family moves again, back to Pisa. Leonardo grows to be a young man and works in the family business. But he must travel for his work.

Leonardo loves to travel and is happy to go. He hopes to learn more about the Arabic way of writing numbers on his trip.

In Egypt, another Arab teacher, Ali, shows Leonardo how to add without an abacus.

Ali explains, "First, write the numbers one above the other, lining up the places in order."

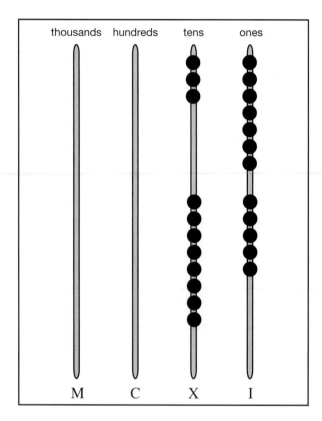

thousands	hundreds	tens	ones
M	C	X	I

"That's just like using an abacus," says Leonardo. "We use pebbles to show the numbers we are going to add. This is how to show thirty-seven and eighty-five on an abacus. Your way looks interesting. What do we do next?"

"Next, we add the 5 and the 7. That makes twelve. But remember, twelve is really one ten and two ones," explains Ali. "So, we write the '2' below the line in the ones place and put the '1' in the tens place above the line."

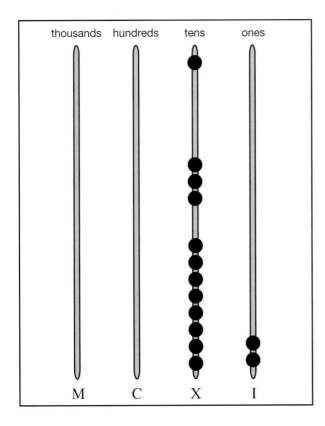

"That's like trading pebbles on the abacus," says Leonardo. "We trade ten ones pebbles for one tens pebble."

"Then what do you do?" asks Ali.

"On the abacus, we would have to trade again," says Leonardo, "since there are too many on the tens line. We trade ten tens pebbles for one hundreds pebble. So, the answer is one hundred twenty-two."

"What we do is similar," says Ali. "The next thing we do is to add the tens. We have 1 + 3 + 8 tens."

"That's twelve tens," says Leonardo.

"But twelve tens are 10 tens and 2 tens," says Ali. "How much are 10 tens?"

"Ten tens make one hundred," says Leonardo. "Is the hundreds place just to the left of the tens place?"

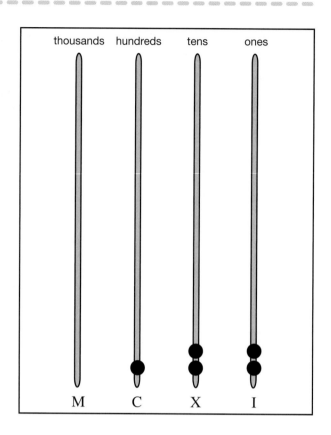

"Yes, exactly. You learn quickly," says Ali. "The 12 tens are 1 hundred and 2 tens, so we put a 1 in the hundreds place and a 2 in the tens place. The answer is 122."

"That's wonderful!" exclaims Leonardo. "Show me another!"

Leonardo quickly learns how to add without an abacus.

Next, he has to go to Syria.

In Syria, Leonardo again meets Arabs who know more mathematics than he does.

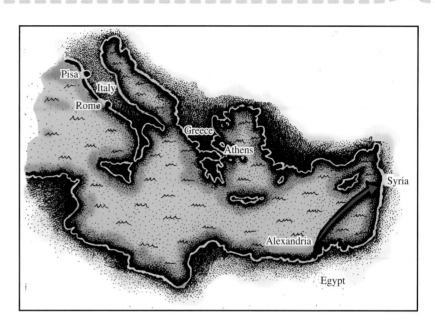

"What if I want to subtract?" asks Leonardo. "How can I do that?"

"Subtraction is a little harder," says Omar, a Syrian mathematician. "But you will learn it if you try."

"The first thing is to write the numbers one above the other, lining up the places."

"Now, you must take the 5 away from the 4," explains Omar.

$$84$$
$$- 25$$

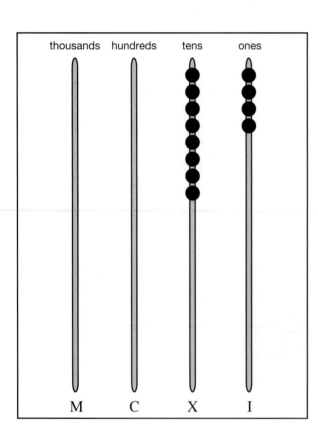

"How can I do that? 5 is more than 4, so it won't work," says Leonardo.

"Think about how you would solve this on an abacus, Leonardo," says Omar. "How would you begin?"

"First, I would put eighty-four on the abacus," says Leonardo.

"Then, I would try to take away twenty-five. Now, since I can't take away five ones pebbles, I have to trade in a tens pebble," continues Leonardo. "So, my abacus looks like this."

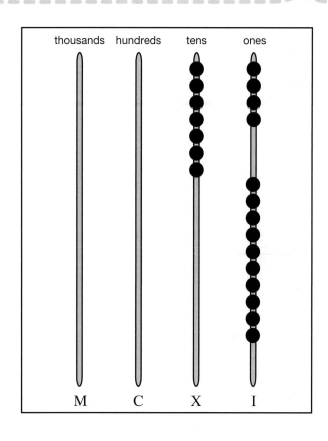

"That's right," says Omar. "Then what would you do?"

"Then, I take away twenty-five," says Leonardo. "That's five ones pebbles and two tens pebbles. That leaves 5 tens pebbles and 9 pebbles, 59."

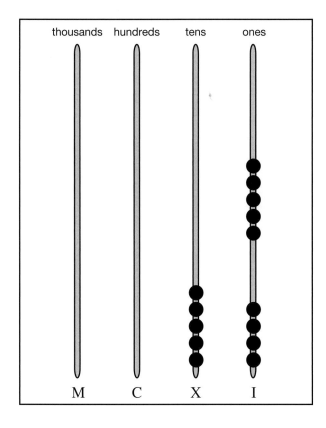

"With these numbers, we do something similar," says Omar. "First, we have to trade. Do you remember what the 8 really means?"

"The 8 is really 8 tens. Oh, I see! We can trade one of the 8 tens for 10 ones. That is just like what we do with the pebbles on an abacus," says Leonardo. "But how do we write that?"

"Just cross out the 8, and write '7' above it. We do this because we have 7 tens left when we trade in 1 of our 8 tens," explains Omar. "That ten plus the 4 ones is 14 altogether, so cross out the 4 and write '14' above it."

"Now, you can subtract the 5. What is 14 minus 5?" asks Omar.

"Nine," answers Leonardo. "Do I write a '9' below the line in the ones place?"

"Yes," says Omar. "Now, can you finish the problem yourself?"

"I think so," says Leonardo. "7 minus 2 is 5. But that's really 7 tens minus 2 tens, so the 5 is really 5 tens. So, I write a 5 in the tens place below the line. The answer is 59, which is the same answer I got with the abacus."

"Very good, Leonardo!" says Omar. "You learn very quickly."

"Thank you," says Leonardo. "But, please, show me some more so I can be sure I understand."

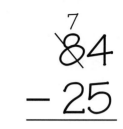

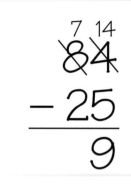

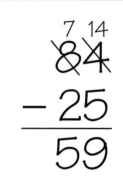

Leonardo spends more time in Syria and travels to Greece as well. Everywhere, he learns more mathematics from the Arabs.

Finally, he goes home. His family is very happy to have him back.

Leonardo is excited about all he has learned and tries to explain it to his father and mother.

"Father," says Leonardo, "we should use the Arabic numerals for our business. They are easier than an abacus. Let me show you how. Suppose we want to add thirty-seven and sixty-eight..."

Leonardo teaches his parents and others how to use the new way of writing numbers.

Soon, Leonardo writes a book of mathematics which he calls *The Book of the Abacus*. He explains the new way of writing numbers and how to use them to add and subtract. He also invents much mathematics of his own. People all over Europe learn from his book.

Leonardo writes many more books of mathematics.

Don't be a blockhead!

Sometimes, Leonardo signs his name Leonardo Bigollo.

This can mean two things, Leonardo the Traveler or Leonardo the Blockhead. Today, people think Leonardo meant to make a joke. He surely did like to travel, but they think he called himself a blockhead to poke fun at the people who thought he was foolish. He was really one of the greatest mathematicians of his time.

Today, we don't call him Leonardo the Blockhead. We know him as Fibonacci, which means "son of Bonacci."

The Ghost Galleons

In 1622, two great Spanish trading ships called galleons came to North America to trade cloth, furniture, and iron for silver, gold, and tobacco.

The records show that they first visited Portobelo in Central America, then went to Cartagena in South America, and finally sailed on to Havana in the Caribbean.

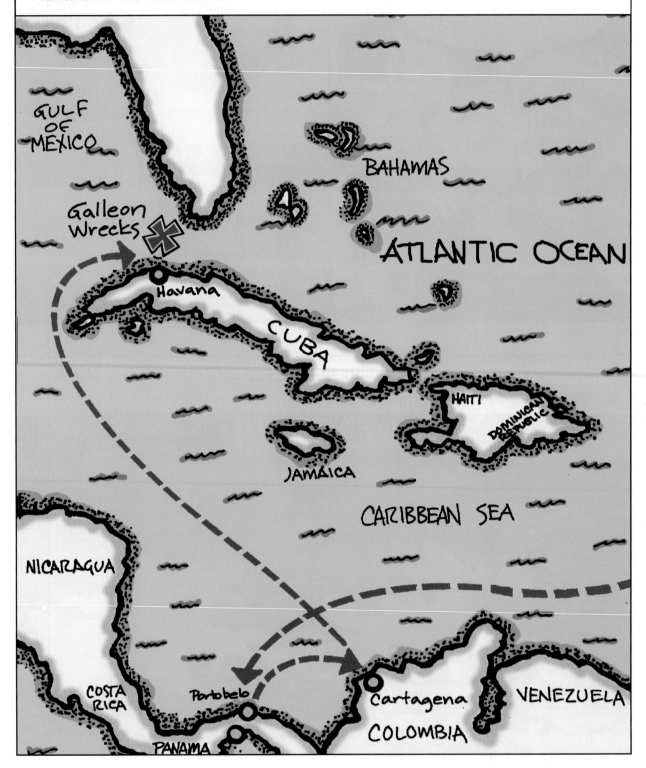

The two ships, the Atocha and the Santa Margarita, arrived in Havana in August. They picked up more silver, gold, and people.

We are carrying 419 silver ingots, 118,000 silver coins, 1488 ounces of gold, and 34 gold bars, Captain.

What a treasure!

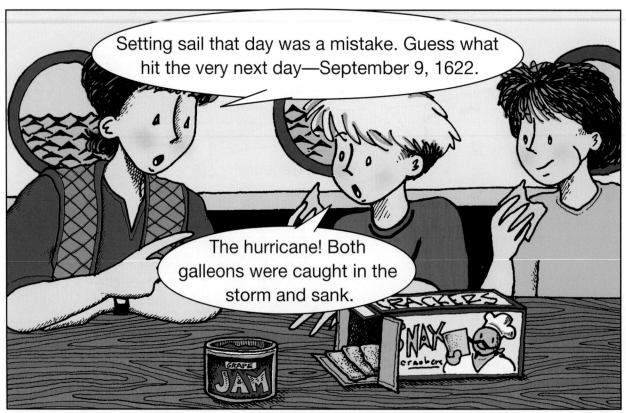

Searching the bottom, they find an anchor!

We found an anchor and broken pottery.

Hooray! Now, we can really hunt. But first, we need to set up a grid so we can make a map.

Using metal pipes, the diving team sets up a grid and explores the area near the anchor.

They find a sword and record its position using a slate that lets them write underwater.

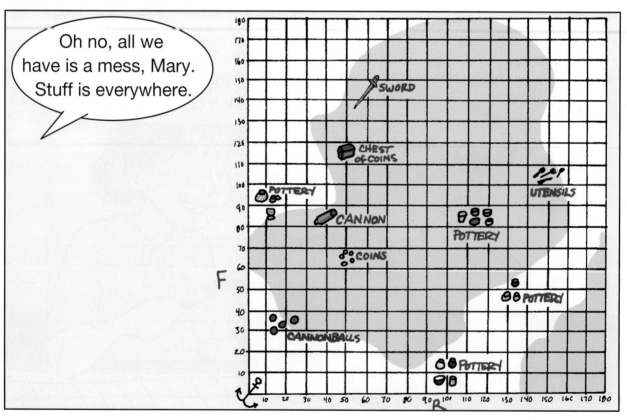

My guess is that these things sank while the ship was moving. The metal things sank quickly and point the direction the ship was going. The pottery and dishes sank slowly, so they were carried by the sea and spread out more.

...they find the broken stern of a ship buried in the mud. It's one of the Ghost Galleons!

They swim inside the old hold of the ship.

Cipher Force!

...56,342 times 0 equals 0...
56,343 times 0 equals 0...
56,344 times 0 equals 0...

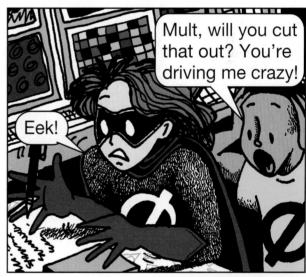

Mult, will you cut that out? You're driving me crazy!

Eek!

Conrad, you know we have to be ready for any problem that might come up.

By working out these answers ahead of time, I'll be prepared for anything.

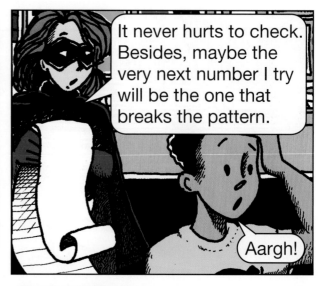

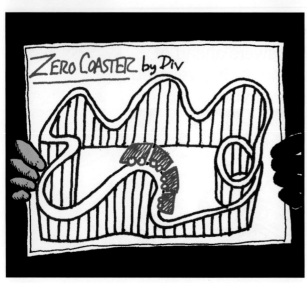

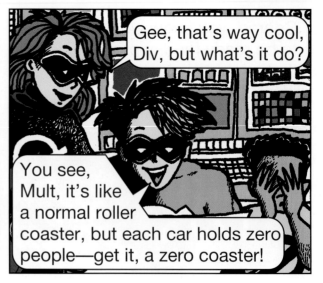

But Div, how can anybody ride it if each car holds zero people?

I figure if I make it long enough it'll work. I've just been working out how many cars a troop of 24 Girl Scouts would fill: 0 girls ride in car 1—only 24 girls are left over; then, 0 more ride in car 2, 24 left, then...

No, no, no, Div! That won't work. Look, suppose you had a regular roller coaster, one that holds four people in each car.

BOR-ing.

Div! I'm trying to explain something to you!

Okay, okay. Go on. Four dull people in each boring car.

Then, to figure out how many cars are needed for 24 Girl Scouts, you have to solve 24 ÷ 4.

"Divide by Four"—big deal. How fascinating.

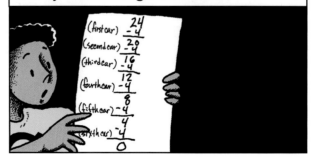

We can work it out by subtraction. Start with 24 Girl Scouts, and subtract 4 for each car. When there are no more left, we'll know how many cars the girls need.

So, 6 cars are enough to hold the 24 girls. 24 ÷ 4 = 6.

Pretty short train. My zero coaster would have a lot more cars for those 24 girls.

That's what I was just figuring out—how many cars long the zero coaster would be for 24 Girl Scouts. Where was I? 0 scouts in car 586, 24 left; 0 scouts in car 587, 24 left…

Div! No matter how many cars…

Just then, Add Zero and Subtract Zero burst in.

Oh, boy.

You'll never guess…

…what we just did.

Tell us! Tell us!

You know General Pillage…

…the company that is burning and bulldozing the rain forest…

…and building toxic waste dumps?

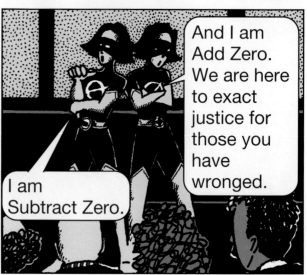

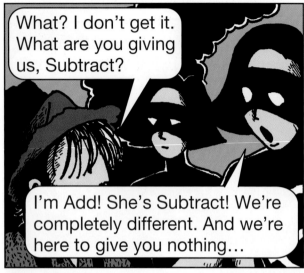

What? I don't get it. What are you giving us, Subtract?

I'm Add! She's Subtract! We're completely different. And we're here to give you nothing…

…and so to help the helpless. We took nothing from General Pillage…

…and now we're here to give it to you. Please take it.

Well, okay, if that's what you want.

Okay.

If you say so.

Glad to be of service. Now, we must be off.

The Cipher Force strikes again.

Boy, are they weird.

It could have been worse. They could have been from General Pillage.

So, I guess we straightened that out, eh, Conrad?

Somehow, I don't think you made much of a difference.

I'll add nothing to our forces! Then, the aliens won't know what hit them.

I'll finish them off none by none. I'll be done in no time!

Good grief!

Don't worry, Conrad, I'll take 'em out: I'll multiply them by zero!

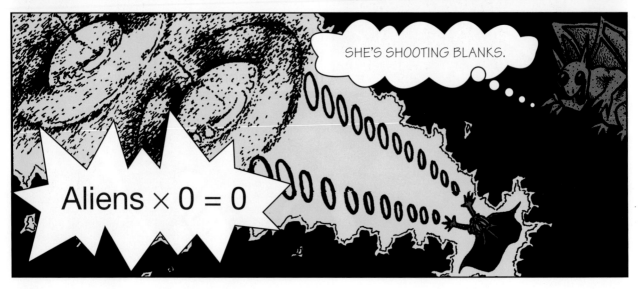

SHE'S SHOOTING BLANKS.

Aliens × 0 = 0

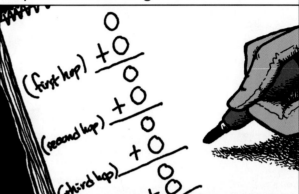

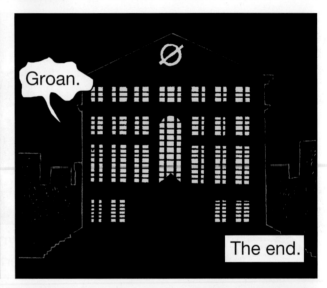

Elixir of Youth
A Sam V. and Tess V. Shovel Mystery

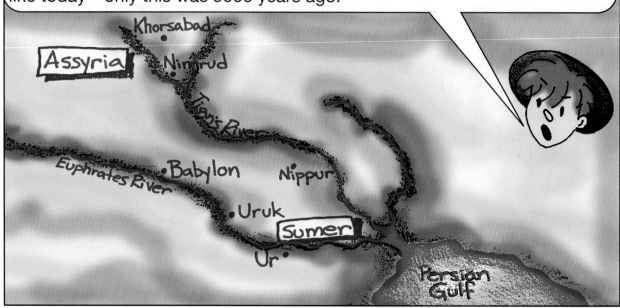

Yes, Tess. The Tigris and Euphrates rivers brought rich soil for crops. The surrounding hills protected the people from invaders. They built cities like Uruk and Ur and developed writing, government, and laws. It was a lot like today—only this was 5000 years ago!

This place is out in the country, Tess.

Great! I love the fresh air!

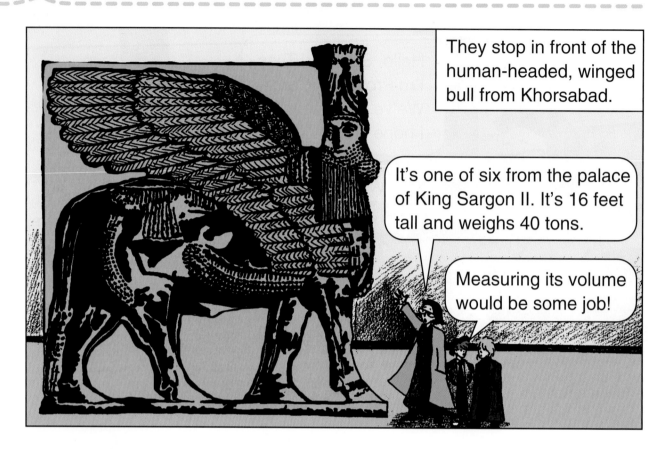

They stop in front of the human-headed, winged bull from Khorsabad.

It's one of six from the palace of King Sargon II. It's 16 feet tall and weighs 40 tons.

Measuring its volume would be some job!

And here is the vase. It's over 4000 years old. It contained an ancient liquid that was supposed to be an elixir of youth. It was tightly sealed.

But the seal's broken, the lid's smashed, and it's empty!

How do you know something was inside?

Sam and Tess find that each bucket can fill five 1-gallon milk containers.

The vase holds 50 buckets and each bucket holds 5 gallons. So, the vase holds 50 × 5 gallons or 250 gallons.

The only clue as to how they got the liquid out is this partly open window. They couldn't go through the front door since somebody might see them. So, it's got to be this window. But it can't go up higher because of the safety bar. So, how did they do it?

Easy! They did just what we did. After they broke the seal, they used a bucket to remove the liquid and filled 1-gallon milk containers. See? The containers just fit.

Great, Tess! But carrying 250 containers isn't easy. Let's look outside.

Sam rushes outside and kneels down by the partly open window.

Tire tracks! These are unusual treads.

Let's check everyone's car!

Then, there's Howard. He's the head of Fundraising and very devoted to the museum. Just last week, I confided in him how desperate I was for an idea to fund this Sumerian exhibit. He promised to do whatever he could to help. No, it couldn't have been Howard.

Tanya is the only other employee who can use the car. She reads ancient writing. I think she drove it last. She took it to a meeting on Monday. She works hard for us. I can't imagine her doing anything like this.

Then, between February 5 and February 14, the car was driven 240 miles on 12 gallons of gas.

How many miles did it go on one gallon? Let's see. How many times does 12 go into 240?

Well, 12 goes into 24 twice, so it goes into 240 20 times. That's 20 miles per gallon. The thief used 4 gallons, so he must have gone 80 miles.

So, the thief drove 80 miles. He or she must have driven to the museum in a car, taken the wagon, and loaded up 250 gallons of elixir in 1-gallon containers. Then, the thief drove to the hiding place, unloaded the containers, and returned the wagon.

Right. So, we know the hiding place must be about 40 miles away!

Boy, you guys are smart! It sure pays to know your volume!

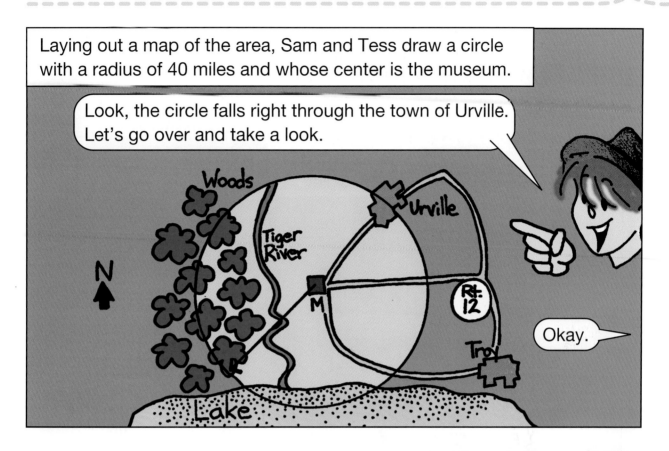

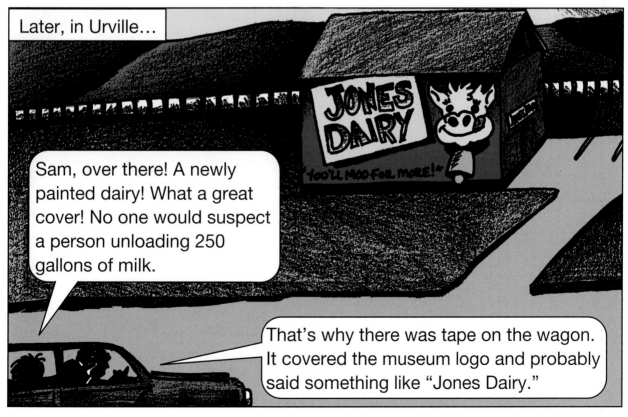

The Clever Tailor (or Three-fourths at One Blow)

Once upon a time, a poor little tailor was sitting in her room sewing a dress for a fine lady.

The work was hard, and the tailor was looking forward to her lunch of bread and jam.

But some flies also wanted the bread and especially the jam. They were buzzing all around the poor tailor's lunch. So, she grabbed her meterstick and struck a mighty blow at the flies.

One fly got away, but she killed three.

"Oh, ho!" cried the tailor. "I have killed three-fourths of these flies with one blow! I am so strong! Three-fourths at one blow! What a hero I am!"

"Why should I be a tailor anymore? I will go into the world and seek my fortune," declared the tailor. "But first, I will make a sash so everyone will know who I am. I will sew 'Three-fourths at One Blow!' on the sash. Then, people will respect and fear me."

So, the tailor made a sash with the words "Three-fourths at One Blow!" on it. She looked around her little room one last time and picked up her meterstick.

"This may be useful," she said.

She also took a piece of bread and her whistle. Then, our brave little tailor went forth into the world to seek her fortune.

She had not gone far when she met a huge and ugly giant.

"Who are you, little girl?" cried the giant in a voice like thunder. Then, he saw the sash. "Three-fourths at One Blow!" read the giant.

"You must be a great fighter. Come, maybe we can be friends."

But the tailor said, "I don't think I can be friendly with such a weak and puny man. Be careful with me, for I have killed three-fourths with one blow."

But the giant did not think he was weak and puny.

"Look, you," he said. "I can eat half of this loaf of bread in one bite. No little person can do that."

"That is nothing. Anybody can eat half in one bite," said the tailor. "Watch what someone who has killed three-fourths with one blow can do. Watch me eat two-thirds of this slice of bread in one bite."

Then, the tailor ate two-thirds of her slice of bread in one bite. And the giant was afraid.

Next, the giant said, "Look how high I can jump. I can jump three-fourths as high as that tree."

He showed her. But again, the tailor did not care.

"Look, you," said the tailor. "Show me something good or I will be angry. Watch how high I can jump. I can jump nine-tenths as high as this meterstick."

Then, the tailor did jump nine-tenths as high as her meterstick. And the giant was even more afraid.

"Watch out! Don't you try to hurt me," cried the giant. "I have ten brothers. If I blow this horn, nine-tenths of them will come at once. They will make you sorry."

"What? You dare to threaten one who has killed three-fourths with one blow?" asked the tailor. "I will blow my whistle, and **all** my sisters will come. Then, I think I will not be the one who is sorry."

Now, the tailor had no sisters, but the giant didn't know that. So, he was very afraid.

"Please, Ma'am," begged the giant, "don't hurt me. Please don't blow your whistle. I was only joking. Here, let's be friends. I have $100—you can have half."

"You should know better than to try to scare one who has killed three-fourths at one blow," said the tailor. "You are foolish, but I forgive you. But you must give me nine-tenths of your money."

So, the giant gave the tailor the money. And the tailor went on her way again.

Soon, the tailor came upon three brothers who were arguing.

"Father said to share the land fairly!" shouted one.

"But this is fair!" said another. "I get one-half, and you each get one-fourth. Then, we each get one piece. That's fair."

"No! That's not fair!" shouted the third brother.

The brothers saw the tailor and took notice of her sash.

"Look!" said the oldest. "Here is a great hero who has killed three-fourths at one blow. Perhaps she can help us."

"Please, Ma'am," said the youngest brother. "Can you help us divide our land fairly?"

"I will try," said the brave little tailor. "Tell me, what is the land like? How big is it?"

"Our land is a rectangle that is 600 meters wide and 300 meters long," explained the middle brother as he drew a picture in the dirt with a stick.

"Now, my older brother wants to divide it like this," he continued, "but my younger brother and I don't think that's fair."

"I don't think it's fair either," said the tailor.

"But each of us gets one piece," said the oldest brother. "What could be more fair than that?"

"I think you need to make the pieces the same size," said the tailor. "Like this." The tailor drew this picture in the dirt.

"Now that's fair!" cried the two younger brothers.

The oldest brother had to agree. The three brothers were so happy to stop arguing that they gave the tailor $10.

"Thank you very much," said the brave little tailor. "Now, I must be on my way."

The tailor's road soon took her deep into a lonely forest. Huge trees blocked out the sun, and not one noise could be heard—not a bird singing, not even an insect buzzing.

All of a sudden, eight nasty-looking robbers leaped out of the bushes and surrounded the brave little tailor.

"Your money or your life!" screamed the meanest looking robber.

But some of the other robbers could read. They noticed the tailor's sash.

"What does that mean?" one robber asked. "Three-fourths at One Blow! Does that mean you can kill three-fourths of us with one blow?"

"How many of us is three-fourths?" asked another robber.

"Would you like to find out?" asked the tailor angrily. "I can show you right now if you want."

"No! No! Don't do that!" cried the robbers. "Calm down. We mean no harm."

"Well, that's better," said the tailor. "I mean no harm either, but you look poor. Do you need money?"

"We dress in these clothes to disguise ourselves," answered the robbers' leader. "Really, we are rich. We each have $1000 with us right now."

"Let's be friends then," said the tailor. "I have some money, too. To show our friendship, let's share our money. I will give you half of my money, and you give me half of yours."

"That's a wonderful idea!" said the leader.

So, the robbers each gave half of their money to the brave tailor. She gave half of her money to the leader of the robbers to share with the others.

The little tailor then went on her way. Now in those days, a dollar was worth far more than it is today. When the little tailor stopped to count her money, she had a big surprise.

"Oh, my!" she exclaimed. "$4050! What a lot of money! Now, I can buy a fine house in the city. I will have a grand life and live all my days happily."

And that's just what she did.

But what about those robbers, the ones who traded half of their money for half of the brave little tailor's money?

They were not doing quite so well.

"What do you mean, $50?" asked one of the band.

"That was her half of the money," said the leader. "We traded half of our money for half of her money."

"And now we have less money?" asked another robber.

"Well, yes, it looks that way," said the leader.

"What a bunch of blockheads we are!" said another. "Well, we can at least share the $50. What is one-eighth of 50?"